Where do rainbows end?

Disney BOOKS BY MAIL

DK Direct Limited
Managing Art Editor Eljay Crompton
Senior Editor Rosemary McCormick
Writer Alexandra Parsons
Illustrators The Alvin White Studios and Richard Manning
Designers Amanda Barlow, Wayne Blades, Veneta Bullen,
Richard Clemson, Sarah Goodwin, Diane Klein, Sonia Whillock

Contents

How do we know what the weather will be?

Because weather scientists have special equipment that can measure all sorts of things we can't see. Scientists can measure how much moisture there is in the air to find out if rain is coming. They have thermometers to tell how hot or cold it is. Even with all their equipment, sometimes scientists still get it wrong!

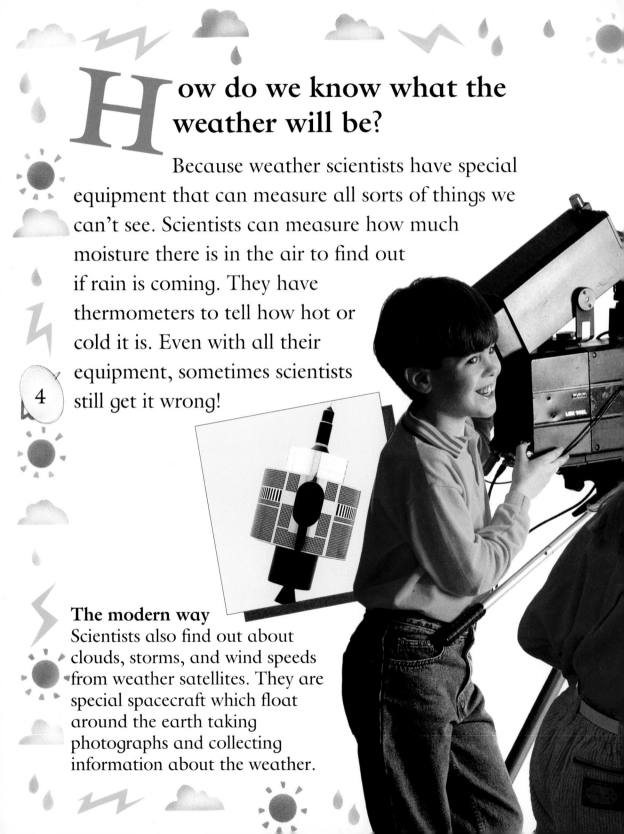

The modern way

Scientists also find out about clouds, storms, and wind speeds from weather satellites. They are special spacecraft which float around the earth taking photographs and collecting information about the weather.

Nature's way

Long ago, people learned that nature gives a lot of clues about the weather. Take your umbrella if you see that pine cones are all closed up, or if cows are lying down in the fields.

If the sky is red in the evening, and if crickets are chirping loudly, then don't forget your sunglasses.

What are thunder and lightning?

They are the sounds and sights of an electric storm. Inside a thundercloud very strong air currents throw ice crystals and water drops around and smash them together. This strong movement fills the crystals and drops with electricity. Electric sparks, or lightning, shoot through the cloud or flash to the ground. This makes the air so hot it pops like a bursting balloon – making thunder.

6

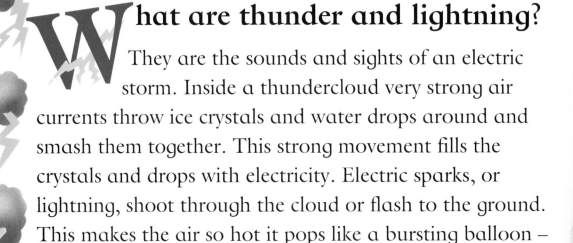

Take care!
Lightning that zig-zags to Earth is called fork lightning. It can be dangerous if it hits people, trees, or buildings.

Simply shocking
What did the thundercloud say to the lightning?
Don't be so flashy!

Crash, bang, flash facts

You can figure out how far away a storm is by counting the number of seconds between the lightning and thunder. Five seconds means a mile.

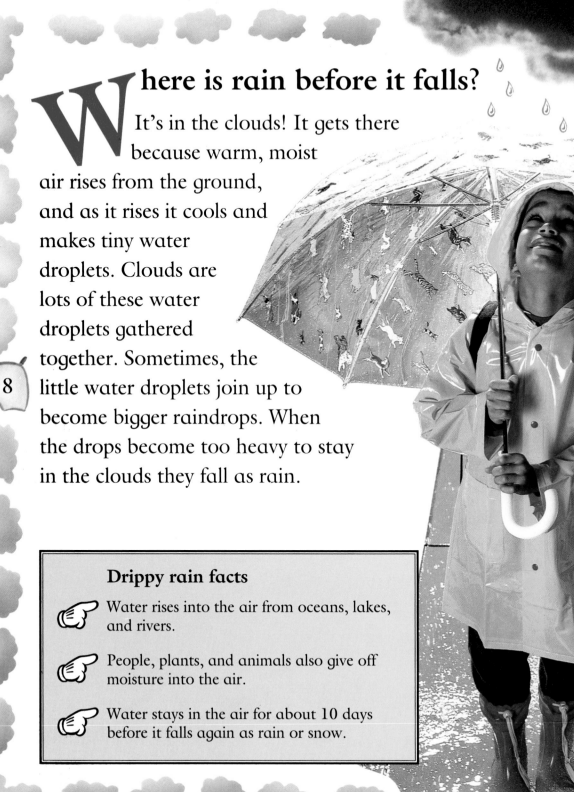

Where is rain before it falls?

It's in the clouds! It gets there because warm, moist air rises from the ground, and as it rises it cools and makes tiny water droplets. Clouds are lots of these water droplets gathered together. Sometimes, the little water droplets join up to become bigger raindrops. When the drops become too heavy to stay in the clouds they fall as rain.

8

Drippy rain facts

☞ Water rises into the air from oceans, lakes, and rivers.

☞ People, plants, and animals also give off moisture into the air.

☞ Water stays in the air for about 10 days before it falls again as rain or snow.

Black and white

Little fluffy clouds don't have much water in them so they look white. Big thick clouds are so full of raindrops they look black. That's because no light can shine through them.

Where do rainbows end?

They don't really end anywhere! In fact, if you were in a plane and looked down at a rainbow, you'd see a circle of color. We see rainbows when the sun shines on falling raindrops. The raindrops reflect the sun's light – which is made of many wonderful colors. As the sunlight passes through the raindrops, it splits up into bands of color.

Beautiful colors
The colors of a rainbow are always in the same order – red, orange, yellow, green, blue, indigo, and violet.

Rainbow magic

 In Ireland people used to say there was a magic pot of gold at the end of every rainbow. But of course you can't find the end of a rainbow – so no one will ever know if it's true or not!

A colorful surprise
What kind of bow is impossible to tie?
A rainbow!

What is wind?

Wind is air moving. Sometimes it moves very slowly and we feel a nice, soft breeze. When it moves more quickly it can become a gale or even a hurricane. In the strongest winds, air is moving faster than a racing car!

Wind at work

People have learned to put the wind to work. In California, there are wind farms where thousands of wheels with blades on them spin around. This spinning energy from the wind is turned into electricity.

Wild, windy facts

☞ Winds are named for the direction they're coming from. So, a wind that comes from the east is called an easterly wind.

☞ Monsoons are winds in tropical places that change direction with the season.

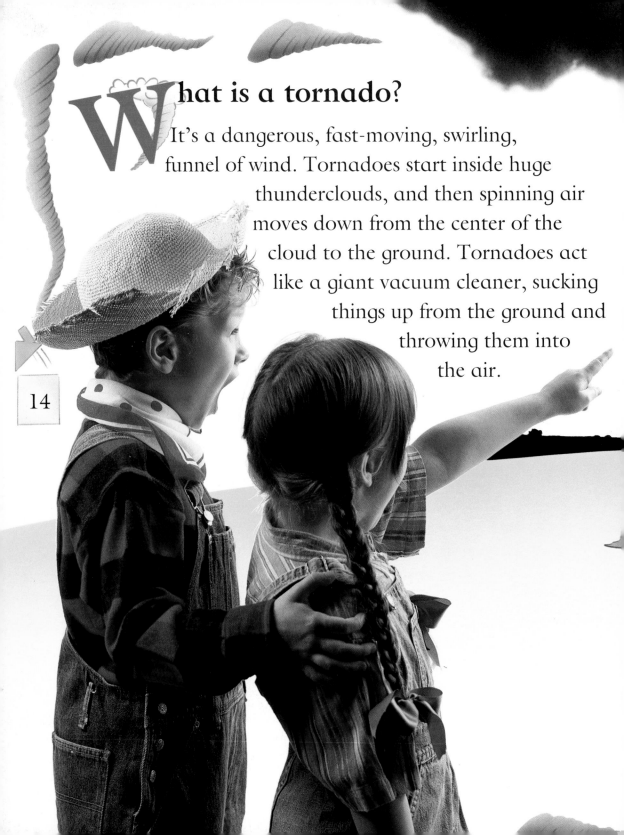

What is a tornado?

It's a dangerous, fast-moving, swirling, funnel of wind. Tornadoes start inside huge thunderclouds, and then spinning air moves down from the center of the cloud to the ground. Tornadoes act like a giant vacuum cleaner, sucking things up from the ground and throwing them into the air.

14

Stormy facts

☞ Tornadoes can move as fast as 300 mph. Some have even moved as fast as 500 mph.

☞ Hurricanes begin as small thunderstorms over warm seas, then pick up speed. They can move as fast as 220 mph.

Hurricane watch
Hurricanes are tropical storms. They are different from tornadoes because the center of a hurricane, which is called the "eye," is calm, but the outside part is very dangerous.

Where does frost come from?

Frost is frozen dew. Dew is the little drops of water you sometimes see on leaves and grass. Dew freezes on cold nights when there are no clouds and no wind. If there were clouds they would act like a blanket, keeping the earth warm. If there were wind, warm and cold air would get mixed up, and it might not get cold enough to make frost.

16

Jack Frost

Long ago, a character called Jack Frost was thought to run his icy fingers over the world and make frost. But we know better!

Frosty patterns

The frost that forms on misty windows is called fern frost.

Frosty facts

☞ Frost can form on airplane wings while planes are flying up high where the air is cold. This can be dangerous, so airplanes have special equipment to get rid of the ice.

☞ Long ago, the weather was much colder in winter than it is now. Rivers froze solid, and people got together and had markets and fairs on the ice.

What is snow made of?

Crystals of ice. Water vapor in clouds freezes into ice crystals. If it is cold enough, the crystals will fall as snow. If it is not quite freezing, the snow crystals will melt and fall as rain.

All snowed up
When a blanket of snow falls it makes everything look different, clean, and new. And it makes everything quieter, too. Snow is like a layer of sound-proofing material.

Pretty crystals

Snowflakes are made of flat crystals. If you looked at a snowflake under a microscope, you would see a six-sided crystal like this. No two snowflakes ever look the same.

Snow ho, ho, ho!
Where do snowmen go to dance?
A snowball!

Snowy things to remember

A blizzard is when it snows and is windy at the same time.

Snow that melts slightly as it falls is called sleet.

The tallest snowman ever built was nearly 67 feet tall – that's as tall as a six story building.

How are icicles made?

They are made when the temperature falls and freezes drops of water and snow that had begun to melt. Icy crystals form and stick to each other. Icicles are usually made on nights when it is very, very cold.

Icing icicles

In Germany, gingerbread houses are made at Christmastime. The walls are cookies, the windows are candy, and the icicles dripping off the roof are made of icing. These are the kind of icicles you SHOULD eat!

Frozen flow

Isn't this amazing? When it gets very, very, very cold, even fast-moving waterfalls freeze solid.

An icy story

 Before refrigerators were invented, farmers used to flood their fields in winter and wait for the water to freeze and turn to ice. Then they cut the ice up into large chunks and took it to the towns. There it was stored in underground ice houses. Now all we have to do is open the refrigerator!

21

Why is the sky blue?

The answer to this question is a little tricky. Sunlight is made up of all the colors of the rainbow. But when it shines on the atmosphere (the thick blanket of air which surrounds the earth), gases in the air bounce mostly blue light toward our eyes.

Red sky at night

Sometimes the sky looks red. This happens when the sun is low in the sky and it shines through thick air. All the other colors get soaked up except for red.

22

Colorful sky facts

In countries close to the north and south poles, spectacular colored lights can sometimes be seen in the sky.

The air doesn't just stop where space begins. It slowly disappears the higher up you go, until there is no air left.

What is fog?

It is a cloud that is close to the ground. And a cloud is a mass of watery mist. Fog happens when very damp air settles close to the ground, and stays there. There is often fog early in the morning before the sun has had a chance to warm the damp air and make it rise.

Smoggy air
Smog happens when the air gets filled up with dust and soot and becomes thick and black and very unhealthy to breathe.

Foggy facts

☞ Lights aren't much
use in thick fog
because they can't be
seen clearly. So some
lighthouses have sirens
and loud foghorns to
warn ships if there is
danger.

What happens in a drought?

When it hasn't rained for a long time, the ground gets very dry. All the water that had collected in rivers, lakes, and reservoirs starts to dry up because heat from the sun causes it to rise as vapor. This is called evaporation. If the drought goes on for a long time, even underground water dries up.

No water, no food

A drought can be a serious problem for farmers. There is less drinking water for farm animals, and sometimes fields dry up and crops die.

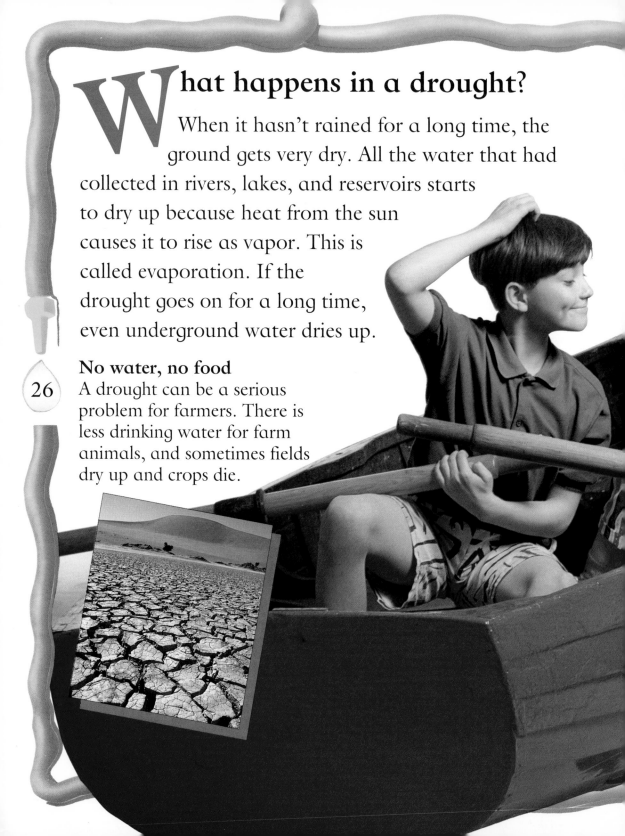

Drought emergency!

☞ We need water for many things. But when there's a drought people are asked to help save water. Can you think of ways to use less water? Here are a few ideas to get you started:

☞ Don't leave the water running while you brush your teeth.

☞ Take quick showers instead of baths.

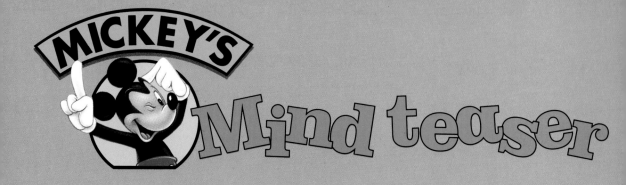

Only one of these rainbows shows the colors of a rainbow in the correct order. Do you know which one it is?

Answer: 2